The Our Father
in
Gethsemane

Thoughts for the Holy Hour

⊳─⊷─O─⊶─⊲

The Our Father in Gethsemane

Thoughts for the Holy Hour

>−I−◆>−O−<◆−I−≺

TAN Books
Charlotte, North Carolina

Nihil Obstat: Arthur J. Scalan, S.T.D.,
                  Censor Librorum.

Imprimatur: ✠ Patrick Cardinal Hayes
                  Archbishop of New York.

New York, October 2, 1935

Originally published in 1935 by William J. Hirten Co., Inc., New York, New York. Typeset and republished in 2010 by TAN Books, Charlotte, North Carolina.

ISBN: 978-0-89555-264-8

Cover design: Lauren A. Rupar.

Cover image: Rome, Italy, Scala Santa. Statue sculpted by Ignazio Jacometti (1854), Jesus Christ praying before his capture. Photo copyright © Paolo Gaetano, iStockphoto.

Printed and bound in the United States of America.

TAN Books
Charlotte, North Carolina

2010

Praeceptis salutaribus moniti
Et divina institutione formati
Audemus dicere

      Pater Noster

Counsels for our good have enlightened us
And the teaching of God has schooled us,
And so we make bold to say,

      Our Father.

      CANON OF THE MASS

HESE thoughts for the Holy Hour (see Appendix) are a development of the Our Father, as the writer's *Holy Hour in Gethsemane* is a development of the *Anima Christi*. The meditations are not directed to the Blessed Sacrament as in *Watching an Hour*, but treat of the sufferings of Our Lord. He is conceived as living and enacting the Our Father in His Agony, and each phrase of Our Lord's Prayer is expanded and applied to the Passion. These meditations appeared originally in the *Messenger of the Sacred Heart* through the kindness of its editor.

It is usual, although not necessary, to have four periods in the Holy Hour, the last quarter given to Benediction or to the Rosary. The other three quarters have each a consideration, a short reflection and a hymn if the hour is made in public. The thoughts are here divided into three parts for the convenience of such an arrangement. In private devotions there is no fixed order. The verses interspersed may be grouped if sung in public. They are all written in the measure of *Tantum Ergo* and may be sung to its airs or to other similar airs. The ejaculations and prayers on the inserted leaves are all indulgenced and are taken from the *Raccolta*.

The book is suited to mental prayer, to visits to the Blessed Sacrament and to Mass.

There have been many developments of the Our Father. The *Catechism of the Council of Trent* has an excellent discussion and will suggest further thoughts if so desired. Cf. *Translation* by McHugh, O.P. and Callan, O.P. No use of the Catechism has been made here.

Contents

Summary

I   Our Father, Who Art in Heaven
Paternal Love: Father in agonies; Father beginning and ending Passion; Father in death.—*Fraternal Love:* Brother in manhood, in Mary, in restored image of God, in parables.—*Eternal Love:* Heaven won by Jesus, lifting the Redeemed to God but denying Himself the beatific vision through life.

II   Hallowed Be Thy Name
By All: By Heaven, by Mary in Magnificat, by the Passion, by the good Thief and by all followers of Jesus.—*In All:* By Jesus, day and night, in every act. *Above All:* Above human pride, above the pain of humiliation, above shattering disappointments.

III   Thy Kingdom Come
Cause of the King: The Kingdom is lovable, is precious, is justly due. — *Conquest of the King:* Kingdom won with the fortitude of Jesus, under the Standard of His Heart, through

victorious prayer.—*Character of the King:* Kingdom by right of inheritance and ownership, by right of all kingly virtues, by the cooperation of followers.

IV   Be It Done

Fiat of Creation: God's making of the world, of bodies and souls, calls for obedience; Jesus obeys in body by pain and in soul by fulfilling God's Commandments.—*Fiat Of Redemption:* Jesus fulfills God's will generously and overflowing for justice and exemplifies the counsels for love.—*Fiat of Sanctification:* The Holy Spirit sums up sanctity in God's will, exemplifies sanctity in Jesus suffering, consoles sanctity by His Presence, as He did in Mary's *Fiat*.

V   Thy Will Be Done on Earth as It Is in Heaven

The Ideal: Jesus fulfills the will of God in His Incarnation, His life, His death; Jesus asks in return gratitude, reparation, love.—*The Ideal Realized:* Heaven realizes God's will in glorified bodies, in glorified souls, in the white sanctity of those saved by Jesus.—*The Real Idealized:* Man's thoughts mind, will, heart and all actions are idealized by being formed like those of Jesus in Agony.

VI   Give Us This Day
Private Prayer: Jesus model of private prayer of agonizing prayer, of intention and attention in prayer.—*Public Prayer:* On important occasions in the life of Jesus, in the sacramentals and sacraments of the Church, in the Sacrifice of the Mass.—*Persevering Prayer:* With Jesus in weariness of body, in weariness of mind, in weariness of will.

VII   Our Daily Bread
Bread of Body: Praying in need, with meritorius hope in want, with Divine hope in death.—*Bread of Soul:* Praying with faith, which illumines Gethsemane, which sees God in an evil world.—*Bread of the Altar:* Praying with charity, finding in Communion God's Presence, God's Power and God's Perfections and uniting all in the friendship of Jesus.

VIII Forgive Us Our Trespasses
God and Sin: Malice of sin proportioned to nearness and to excellence of the person offended; Agony of Jesus proportioned to malice of sin. — *Man-God and Sin:* Jesus suffers in agony for original sin, for venial, sins for mortal sins. — *Man and Sin:* Justice of forgiveness, fullness of forgiveness, joy of forgiveness.

IX As We Forgive Our Trespassers
Jesus Preaches Forgiveness: Forgiveness a characteristic Christian virtue, a measure of our forgiveness an act of perfect mercy. — *Jesus Practices Forgiveness:* His forgiveness is prompt and full, extends to sinful woman and doubting apostle and embraces the Traitor Judas. — *Jesus Perfects Forgiveness.*

X And Lead Us not into Temptation
Our Weakness: Strength for weakness of body, for weakness of mind, for weakness of will. — *Our Watchfulness:* Watching outwardly against occasion of sin, watching inwardly against weak habits by prayers. — *Our For-*

titude: From the angel of the Agony, from the example of Jesus in His temptation and in His Agony.

XI   But Deliver Us From Evil
Deliverance by Faith: Faith finds good in evil, and sees Jesus with us in our Gethsemane and in our crucifixions. — *Deliverance by Character:* Character with the fortitude of Christ bears sufferings, seeks sufferings, loves sufferings. — *Deliverance by Holiness:* Christ's temperance delivers the body; His prudence delivers the mind: His justice delivers the will.

XII   So Be It
Amen of Men: Amen resumes the whole prayer, ratifies all conclusions, attests the sincerity of all resolves. — *Amen of Jesus:* His amen is an assurance of truth, an invitation to prompt obedience, a testimony sealed with blood. — *Amen of God:* Eternally glorifying man's body, soul and love.

Texts

"Thus therefore shall you pray: Our Father who art in Heaven, hallowed be Thy name. Thy kingdom come. Thy will be done on earth as it is in Heaven. Give us this day our daily bread. And forgive us our trespasses as we also forgive those who trespass against us. And lead us not into temptation. But deliver us from evil. *Amen.*"

"And going out, he went according to his custom to the Mount of Olives. And his disciples also followed him. And when he was come to the place, he said to them: Pray lest ye enter into temptation. And He was withdrawn away from them a stone's cast, and kneeling down He prayed, saying: Father, if Thou wilt, remove this chalice from Me, but yet not My will but Thine be done. And there appeared to him an angel from Heaven, strengthening him. And being in agony, he prayed the longer. And his sweat became as drops of blood, trickling down upon the ground. And when he rose up from prayer and was come to his disciples, he found them sleeping for sorrow. And he said to them: Why sleep you? Arise, pray lest you enter into temptation."

Paraphrases

The following paraphrase composed by St. Francis of Assisi is cited by A. Lapide, *Matt. 6, 13* and praised as "sublime, full of unction and of fervor."

Our most holy *Father*, Creator, Redeemer, Sanctifier and Consoler, *who art in Heaven*, with angels and saints, enlightening them with a knowledge of Thyself, because Thou, Lord, art light, enkindling in them the flame of divine love; because Thou, Lord, art love, dwelling in them and filling them with eternal happiness; because Thou, Lord, art the highest good and everlasting good, from whom is all good and without whom there is no good.

Hallowed be Thy name! May the knowledge of Thee grow brighter within us to comprehend what is the extent of Thy blessings, the duration of Thy promises, the sublimity of Thy majesty and the profundity of Thy judgments!

Thy kingdom come, that Thou mayst reign within us by Thy grace and bring us to Thy kingdom, where there is clear vision of Thee, perfect love of Thee, blessed companionship with Thee, unending enjoyment of Thee!

Thy will be done on earth as it is in Heaven, that we may love Thee with our whole heart in always thinking of Thee, with our whole soul in always desiring Thee, with our whole mind in directing all our intentions to Thee and in seeking Thy glory in everything, and with all our strength by displaying all our powers and the vigor of soul and body in devotion to Thy love above everything else: that we may love our neighbors as ourselves by bringing all men, as far as we can, to the love of Thee, by rejoicing in the good fortune of others as we do in our own, by sympathy with them in their sorrows and by giving offence to no one!

Give us this day our daily bread. Give us this day Thy beloved Son, Our Lord Jesus Christ, in our memory in our mind and in homage to the love which He manifested towards us and in homage to all His deeds, words and sufferings:

And forgive us our trespasses through Thy mercy, through the marvelous efficacy of the Passion of Thy beloved Son, Our Lord Jesus Christ and through the merits and prayers of Blessed Mary, the Virgin and of all the elect!

As we forgive those who trespass against us, and because we fail to forgive fully, do

Thou, Lord, make us forgive fully, loving our enemies for Thy sake, praying to Thee earnestly for them, returning not evil for evil but zealously striving with Thy help to do good to all!

And lead us not into temptation, hidden or manifest, sudden or oppressive!

But deliver us from evil, past, present and future!

Amen, freely and generously!

Purgatory Canto XI

"Our Father, who art in Heaven,—indeed thereby
Not circumscribed, but for the greater love
Thou hast for Thy first handiwork on high,—
Hallowed be Thy name and excellence
By every creature, even as it is meet
To render thanks for Thy sweet effluence.
Thy kingdom come of peace, for unto it,
Unless it come to us, not of ourselves
Can we attain, whatever be our wit.
As of their will Thy angels make to Thee
Their joyful sacrifice, singing Hosanna,
So may men make of theirs as joyfully.
Give us this day our daily bread of grace,
Without which through this bitter wilderness
He backward goes who most would on apace.
And as we pardon to each one the hurt
Which we have suffered, do Thou, merciful,
So may men make of theirs as joyfully.
Our virtue which is light to overthrow,
Put not to proof with the old Adversary,
But keep it safe from him, who spurs it so.
This last petition is, dear Lord, designed
Not for ourselves, who have thereof no need
But for the ones who linger still behind."

THE DIVINE COMEDY OF DANTE, TRANSLATED BY JEFFERSON
BUTLER FLETCHER; THE MACMILLAN CO., NEW YORK.

"Mental Sufferings of Our Lord in His Passion"

THERE, then, in that most awful hour, knelt the Saviour of the world, putting off the defences of His divinity, dismissing His reluctant Angels, who in myriads were ready at His call, and opening His arms, baring His chest, sinless as He was, to the assault of His Foe—of a foe whose breath was a pestilence, and whose embrace was an agony. There He knelt, motionless and still, while the vile and horrible fiend clad His spirit in a robe steeped in all that is hateful and heinous in human crime, which clung close round His heart, and filled His conscience, and found its way into every sense and pore of His mind, and spread over him a moral leprosy, till He almost felt Himself to be that which He never could be, and which His foe would fain have made Him. Oh, the horror when He looked, and did not know Himself, and felt as a foul and loathsome sinner, from His vivid perception of that mass of corruption which poured over His head and ran down even to the skirts of His garments!

Oh, the distraction, when He found His eyes, and hands, and feet, and lips, and heart, as if the members of the Evil One, and not of God! Are these the hands of the Immaculate Lamb of God, once innocent, but now red with ten thousand barbarous deeds of blood? are these His lips, not uttering prayer, and praise, and holy blessings, but as if defiled with oaths, and blasphemies, and doctrines of devils? or His eyes, profaned as they are by all the evil visions and idolatrous fascinations for which men have abandoned their adorable Creator? And His ears, they ring with the sounds of revelry and of strife; and His heart is frozen with avarice, and cruelty, and unbelief; and His very memory is laden with every sin which has been committed since the fall, in all regions of the earth, with the pride of old giants, and the lust of the five cities, and the obduracy of Egypt, and the ambition of Babel, and unthankfulness and scorn of Israel. Oh, who does not know the misery of a haunting thought which comes again and again, in spite of rejection, to annoy, if it cannot seduce? or of some odious and sickening imagination, in no sense one's own, but forced upon the mind

from without? or of evil knowledge, gained
with or without a man's fault, but which he
would give a great price to be rid of at once
and forever?

And adversaries such as these gather
around Thee, Blessed Lord, in millions now;
they come in troops more numerous than the
locust or the palmer-worm, or the plagues
of hail, and flies, and frogs, which were sent
against Pharaoh. Of the living, of the dead
and of the as yet unborn, of the lost and of the
saved, of Thy people and of strangers, of sinners and of saints, all sins are here. Thy dearest are there; Thy saints and Thy chosen are
upon Thee: Thy three apostles, Peter, James,
and John; but not as comforters, but as accusers, like the friends of Job, "sprinkling dust
towards Heaven," and heaping curses on Thy
head. All are there but one; one only is not
there, one only; for she who had no part in sin,
she only could console Thee, and therefore she
is not nigh. She will be near Thee on the Cross,
she is separated from Thee in the Garden. She
has been Thy companion and Thy confidant
through Thy life. She interchanged with Thee
the pure thoughts and holy meditations of

thirty years; but her virgin ear may not take in, nor may her immaculate heart conceive, what now is in vision before Thee. None was equal to the weight but God; sometimes before Thy Saints Thou hast brought the image of a single sin, as it appears in the light of Thy countenance, or venial sins, not mortal; and they told us that the sight all but killed them, nay, by reason of it, could not have borne one brood of that innumerable progeny of Satan which now compasses Thee about.

It is the long history of the world, and God alone can bear the load of it. Hopes blighted, vows broken, lights quenched, warnings scorned, opportunities lost; the innocent betrayed, the young hardened, the penitent relapsing, the just overcome, the aged failing; the sophistry of misbelief, the willfulness of passion, the obduracy of pride, the tyranny of habit, the canker of remorse, the wasting fever of care, the anguish of shame, the pining of disappointment, the sickness of despair; such cruel, such pitiable spectacles, such heart-rending, revolting, detestable, maddening scenes; nay, the haggard faces, the convulsed lips, the flushed cheeks, the dark brow of the willing slaves of evil, they are all before Him now; they are upon Him and in Him. They are with Him instead of that ineffable peace which has inhabited His soul since the moment of His conception. They are upon Him, they are all but His own; He cries to His Father as if He were a criminal, not the victim; His agony takes the form of guilt and compunction. He is doing penance. He is making confession, He is exercising contrition, with a reality and a virtue infinitely greater than that of all the saints and penitents together; for He is the One Victim for us all, the sole satisfaction, the real Penitent, all but the real sinner.

Newman: *Sermons for Mixed Congregations*.

OUR FATHER, WHO ART IN HEAVEN

Our Father, Who Art in Heaven
Pater Noster Qui Es in Coelis

Paternal Love

PATER. When you enter upon your agonies, which are piercing enough for you, however slight they may be when compared with the Agony of Jesus, what prayer above all will you whisper with anguished heart? Should it not be the prayer the Lord has taught us, the prayer which He may be said to have lived in deed before He put it into words, the prayer that He enacted within His Heart in the garden of Mount Olivet, the "Our Father"? Like the hurt child who at once calls to its parent, you will cry "Father" to the God of love. Of old, God was far-off, awesome, mysterious. In the prayer which Jesus taught you, God is near you. Indeed, He feels and suffers like you through the human Heart He took upon becoming man.

It was the "Our Father," you may well believe, that Jesus expressed in His every act and thought and desire when He began His Passion with an hour of prayer. The Church commences prayers, as is quite natural, with an appeal to the one addressed, under a title which is an evidence of trust and grounds for confidence. "Father" is the address on the quivering lips of Jesus; "Father" is the first utterance upon His Cross; "Father" is His last cry, when Jesus commends His soul to God and like a tired child closes His fevered eyes in the sleep of death.

Jesus is preparing to give to you the clearest testimony of His unequaled love, and when overshadowed by approaching death, He turns to Him who is Love Itself, to the Father. There you too will turn when the shadows close in upon you, knowing that the Father's eyes watch you, the Father's hand clasps yours and guides your faltering steps, and through the Heart of Jesus the Father warms your chilled heart. You will find in the Father love Divine and love paternal.

Fraternal Love

POSTER. Jesus, who had the supreme right to say "My Father" in the prayer He gave you, yet chose to say "Our Father."

Jesus there made Himself our Brother, and sealed that adoption by making His Mother our Mother. The vision of His sorrowing Mother made the sorrows of Jesus more bitter, but as His wounds became our healing, so His Cross is our life and blessing. The Passion of Jesus it was which made His Father our Father by making you and me the children of God by Divine adoption. The family likeness given by Creation but marred by the sin of Adam, our earthly father, and by our own sins—that likeness is now restored and made a Divine likeness through the grace of the Redeemer.

You are in the garden beside Jesus when He lives the "Our Father." You are the strayed sheep for whom the Lamb of God is to be sacrificed. You are the lost coin Jesus looks for through the dark night. You are the prodigal whom Jesus is guiding home to the Father waiting in love. You and all cry out with Jesus, not "my Father only, nor "yours" only, but "ours"—wholly to each and wholly to every one. You see the sun by other rays than those which come to my eyes, but we both behold the whole sun in all its golden glory.

Alas, no sun shed its rays upon the darkness of Gethsemane. The night of suffering must precede the day of salvation.

The love of Jesus in His Agony soared to a Divine height, to the Father: His love, following the rays of Bethlehem's star, extended to the measureless width of all mankind, to our Father. As you kneel beside Jesus sorrowing, you will not only cry "Our Father," but will whisper in sympathizing love, "Our Brother." The love of God voiced in the "Our Father" is universally fraternal as well as divinely paternal.

Eternal Love

QUI ES IN COELIS. Jesus might have flooded His soul with the resplendence of Heaven as He did upon Mount Tabor. He was ever in Heaven, although for your sake He did not permit His human nature always to feel and reflect the shining joys of eternity. In His Agony He not only closes out the light of Heaven, but he also admits the blackest darkness of earth. The garments of Jesus are not now white as snow. No, they are dyed with the Blood of the Lamb, that the unnumbered throng of the blessed may make white their garments in the cleansing flood which began its copious gushing in the Agony.

You may have heard of the scientist of old who said that he could lift the whole round earth with a lever if he had a place to stand and rest his lever. Jesus by His wounds and death did far more than that. He lifted the sinful children of Adam, weighted by an oppressive transgression, far up to the bright presence of God and holds them there forever.

But now, alas, Jesus keeps Heaven far from Himself while the process of Redemption goes on. He is now putting wearied and wounded hands to the lever of salvation. The wood which is to lift you from sin and sorrow, the wood upon which the hands of Jesus are laid, is the hard, rough wood of the Cross. Its weight has already in vision begun to press upon His shoulders with sharpened edges. In foreboding terror He already feels in His palms the pointed nails, which are to pierce through on the morrow.

Truly the love of Jesus is paternal in its heavenly height, fraternal in its all-embracing width, and eternal in its glorious duration.

Prayer

Heart of Fatherly Love, agonized for all Thy brethren in the darkness of Mount Olivet, give to the hearts of Thy children a spark of Thy infinite affection, that inflamed with Thy charity in the trials of life, we may forever possess the consolations of our Father who is in Heaven. *Amen.*

OUR FATHER

He whose might keeps worlds obeying.
Fount of nature's myriad powers,
He, as Father, hears our praying;
We, as children, call Him Ours.

>─I─◆─O─◆─I─◄

Omnipotence of the Father, help my frailty, and rescue me from the depths of misery.

Wisdom of the Son, direct all my thoughts, words, and actions.

Love of the Holy Spirit, be the source of all the operations of my soul, so that they may be entirely conformed to the divine will.

"My God and My All!"

"My God, my only good, Thou art all mine; grant that I may be all Thine!"

Hallowed Be Thy Name
Sanctificetur Nomen Tuum

Hallowed By All

SANCTIFICETUR. In Heaven the name of God is blessed and hallowed. The Angels in the Apocalypse "rested not day and night, saying: Holy, holy, holy, Lord God Almighty, who was and who is and who is to come." That is the cry Isaias heard: "Holy, holy, holy, the Lord God of hosts, all the earth is full of His glory."

On earth the holiest of God's creatures, Mary, the Mother of Jesus, echoed the song of Heaven in her *Magnificat* of humble gratitude, thanking God in her "Our Father" hymn, "Because He that is mighty hath done great things to me, and holy is His name."

The greatest hallowing of God's name took place when Jesus went to His Agony and Crucifixion. The simplest act, the briefest thought, the merest wish of Jesus, the Man-God, was enough to give an infinite hallowing, a perfect glory to the Name of all names; but Jesus desired that His entire

25

body with all its acts, his whole mind in every thought, His full Heart in the complete out-pouring of love, should become an offering of sacrifice for the glory of God.

There was an encouraging answer to the prayerful sacrifice of Jesus, when the good thief hallowed on his cross the name of Jesus and was himself hallowed in turn. For a time, however, the followers of Jesus, sleeping, dispersing in fear, denying their Lord, gave but slight comfort to the praying and suffering Saviour. Jesus would have all mankind unite with the Angels in Heaven, with His Mother on earth, with the Christmas song that echoed the *Magnificat*; and by His agonizing prayer He teaches your heart and every heart to hallow God in unison with His heart.

Hallowed in All

OMEN. The hallowing of God's name in the "Our Father" is to be done in all things as well as by all people. Jesus found sermons in God's universe. He crossed the fields, He forded the streams, He climbed the hills, He sailed the

lakes, and every where beheld the vestiges
of God's power in the order, the wisdom, the
beauty of creation. The lilies of the field as well
as the shining stars of the sky hallowed God's
name by reflecting the glory of the Creator.

Jesus went out into the darkness and
went down into the valley of Gethsemane to
hallow the Father's name. Even in the night,
when clouds curtain the stars and blackness
blots out all visions of beauty, "Hallowed be
Thy name," is still the prayer of Jesus. Yes,
in gloom, in pain, in abandonment, in agony
of soul and body, Jesus leads the way for you
that you may still whisper, whatever may
come to you, "Hallowed be Thy name!"

In all places, in all states, and in all
actions, too, glory is to be given to God and
His name is to be hallowed. Every act of
Jesus in His agonized Passion was for you;
every thought was concerned with you. He
became the embodiment of the "Our
Father,"—a living, feeling, suffering prayer—
to win eternal glory for you that you might
hallow the Father's name in your life in word and
deed and thought through the hallowing grace
of Redemption. Could your every movement

of body and soul become vocal and speak, should it not be saying from earliest dawn until the last light of the day and through every breath of the sleeping night, "Hallowed be Thy name!"?

Hallowed Above All

UUM. The name of God signifies the Person of God, the perfections of God: His wisdom, His power, His goodness. Why is it that you must pray that His name be praised and honored? One sad reason is the pride of man. Man is selfish, and in his pride would have all glory for himself. The excellence of God in Himself cannot be increased, but it may be forgotten or disdained by man. So you must put off all pride and put on humility, and pray that God be hallowed not only by all, not only in all, but also above all.

Humiliation is a pain above all pains of body. To be disappointed in self, to be lowered to the dust, inflicts a wound which it is very hard to heal. For years a humiliation leaves a smarting ache, and in many cases it is the forerunner of a nervous breakdown. Not to come up to God's expectations does not depress so much, but to fail to come up to one's own expectations, especially when competing with others—that is anguish. Look then, humiliated heart, at Jesus, who is God, and took upon Himself the form of a slave and humbled Himself to the death of a slave.

If you kneel beside Jesus in the Garden, and go down part way with Him into the dark valley of humiliation, you will not feel the weight of disappointment so keenly or so long. The humiliation which crushed Jesus will lighten and illuminate your heavy gloom. Do you not remember that water sprays to white mist and ice powders to snow and colored glass grinds to white dust and even black ink will dash into white foam? And why? Because from a thousand facets the sunlight, which was not fully reflected in the unshattered substance, flashes white in all the blended colors of the day. Through the humiliation of Jesus your darkened and crushed soul becomes shining white and full of comfort.

Prayer

Jesus, whose every heart-beat, whether of pleasure or of pain, gave the fullest glory to the Father's name, grant, we beg of Thee, that in generous humility we may ever glorify God upon earth, and so merit to be numbered with the Angels in singing glory to God in the highest. *Amen.*

HALLOWED BE THY NAME

Angels through high Heaven's arches,
Thy Name hallowing ever sing;
Let that chanting fill earth's churches
In all hearts reechoing!

I adore Thee. O my God, one God in three Persons; I annihilate myself before Thy Majesty. Thou alone art being, life, truth, beauty, and goodness. I glorify Thee, I praise Thee. I thank Thee, and I love Thee, all incapable and unworthy as I am, in union with Thy dear Son Jesus Christ, our Saviour and our Father, in the mercifulness of his heart and through his infinite merits. I wish to serve Thee, to please Thee, to obey Thee, and to love Thee always, in union with Mary immaculate, Mother of God and our Mother, loving also and serving my neighbor for Thy sake. Therefore, give me Thy Holy Spirit to enlighten, correct, and guide me in the way of Thy commandments, and in all perfection, until we come to the happiness of Heaven, where we shall glorify Thee for ever. Amen.

"God be blessed!"

"Praised be Jesus Christ forever!"

"Sacred Heart of Jesus, be Thou known, be Thou loved, be Thou imitated!"

Thy Kingdom Come
Adveniat Regnum Tuum

Cause of the King

ADVENIAT. That the Kingdom of God might come to all hearts upon earth, Jesus became man. Throughout His teaching the Kingdom is described to you in every form that can win your love. The Kingdom of Heaven is seed and harvest, precious coin and pearl of great price, full lamps and fit raiment for a wedding, the fold for the lost sheep and the home for the prodigal son. You long that all those blessings should come to you, and you join Jesus in Gethsemane when He suffers and prays for every heart in His Agony: Our Father, may Thy Kingdom come!

The Kingdom of God is full of all goodness, as Jesus has told you, and it is also a kingdom of justice. "The Kingdom of God," says St. Paul, "is not meat and drink, but justice and peace and joy in the Holy Ghost." If you have the justice of the Kingdom, you will have its joy and peace. In the pictures of God's Kingdom which Jesus paints in such glowing colors, there is always question of justice: due planting and care of the seeded field, due payments, due prudence and watchfulness, due search for what is lost, and due sorrow of the unjust offender.

It was the justice of God that Jesus upheld as the ideal when he entered upon His public life and told the hesitating Baptist, "It becomes us to fulfil all justice." That is the ideal for the followers of Jesus, who are to hunger and thirst after justice, who are to seek first of all justice, who are to abound in justice more than the enemies of Jesus. It is to satisfy the eternal justice of God that Jesus enters upon His Agony for you and every sinner. Your King has a just cause, the justice of God. May that Kingdom come!

Conquest of the King

REGNUM. The conquest of Jesus, the King, is even more just, if possible, than His cause. The punishment due to you for your sins, Jesus took upon Himself. "He loved me and He delivered Himself up for me." "He was wounded for our iniquities; He was bruised for our sins . . . and by His bruises we are healed." Jesus is truly the Lamb of God, who offered full atonement for the injustice of sin. True it is that "the Kingdom of Heaven suffereth violence and the violent bear it away." You must indeed have fortitude of heart and must suffer that the Kingdom may come to you, but you know that Jesus suffered before you for its coming, and now gives to your pain through His rich merits the power of atoning for yourself and for others.

Jesus showed to you that grief can be made glory, that wounds may be true pledges of lasting health, and that defeat and death can result in life and victory. The Heart which Jesus displays upon His breast is the standard under which He conquered for God's justice. It is a standard which has faced a severe campaign and bears the wound-stripes of supreme service. You see His Heart all aglow with the fiery zeal for God's justice, the zeal which cleansed the temple. You see His Heart bear upon Its tender summit the weighty burden of the Cross. You see that the only armor which protects It is a crown woven of thorny brambles. You note the mute lips which testify that Jesus emptied His Heart to fulfill all justice.

Little wonder that the League of the Sacred Heart takes the petition "Thy Kingdom come!" as its inspiriting war-cry, and makes the wounded Heart of Jesus its standard in its campaign of prayer. Justice reigns now in Heaven through the generous payment of Jesus, but justice has not yet come to its own among men, The Agony of Jesus is suffered that every soul may share in the bountiful and merciful justice of the Saviour. "Thy Kingdom come!" is your prayer from early dawn, the whole day through, and even during the night in restful slumber or restless vigil, persevering with the King in His conflict till the blessings of justice come to all men.

Character of the King

TUUM. The King is more than His cause and His conquest. Jesus has the kingly character. By right of inheritance through God the Father, by right of ownership as Creator, Jesus is your King.

By right of conquest, too, He rules you. When in conflict for God's just cause Jesus raised the standard of His crucified Heart and entered upon the struggle which culminated on Calvary, then Jesus by a new title became King of all hearts. There He reigns through the grace He won in His hard-earned victory.

Jesus has, then, the kingly character and He has, too, the character of a King. Make an inventory of all the virtues which have characterized the leaders of men and won for them a throne and devoted followers, and all those traits fade into darkness when compared with the resplendent excellences found in Jesus. Different leaders have had different good qualities, but Jesus possessed them all in a Divine degree. The wisdom of Solomon, the devotedness of David, the saintliness of the crusading Louis, the courage of a thousand chieftains, are shadows when compared with the Orient on high, Jesus, who is your King.

You, then, will be a crusader for the Kingdom in your own soul. You will associate yourself with your peerless Leader in His conflict. He has trodden the wine-press of Olivet that you may endure the slight pressure of your vintage. You will keep close to Him and thrill to the touch of His hand and feel the warmth of His Heart. Jesus faces the trampling hordes of sin's battalions, and the weight of their onset crushes in a thousand jets as from bursting grapes His sacramental wine. One drop of that saving dew satisfies the justice of God and, like a flake of dye dissolving in water, will color your days with the ardent courage of the crusader for the Kingdom and the King.

Prayer

Jesus, King of Kings, whose Divine right is sanctioned by every title, assist us to pay Thee the due loyalty of true subjects, that with love answering Thy love we may enthrone Thee forever in our hearts. *Amen.*

THY KINGDOM COME

Not for our King jeweled crowning
On a dais, lone, apart;

Give Him love's secure enthroning
And leal royalty of heart.

Eternal Father, we offer Thee the Blood, Passion, and Death of Jesus Christ, and the sorrows of the most holy Mary and St. Joseph, in payment for our sins, in suffrage for the holy souls in purgatory, for the wants of our holy Mother the Church, and for the conversion of sinners. Amen.

"Sacred Heart of Jesus, Thy Kingdom Come!"

"All for Thee, most Sacred Heart of Jesus!"

"Oh, merciful God, grant that I may eagerly desire, carefully search out, truthfully acknowledge and ever perfectly fulfill all things which are pleasing to Thee, to the praise and glory of Thy Name!"

Be It Done

Fiat

Fiat of Creation

IAT. The first manifestation of the will of God to you is in the world about you. "Let the world be made!" was the Fiat of our Father, the Fiat of Creation. At the word of the Creator the universe in obedience sprang straightway into existence. Your food and clothing were at hand. All science in God's truth, all art in God's beauty lay before mankind for their study, and for their enraptured gaze. God gave to the animal kingdom its dress through nature; to men was given a greater gift, the power of reason which enabled men to fashion their own raiment.

But God gave you a still greater gift, the freedom of your will by which you can make the right use of creatures and can govern your body and soul in loving obedience to His Divine will. You are created to the image of God with the power to know Him, to love Him, to serve Him. That is your fiat in response to the Fiat of the Father.

Jesus, entering into His Agony, uttered His obedient submission to the Father, "Not My will but Thine be done! Father, My body is worn out and now must be tortured: Thy will be done! Father, my eyes are darkened now by the gloom of night, but ere long they will be veiled in a cloud of blood: Thy will be done! The way is to be rough for My feet and the burden is to be heavy for My hands; but Thy will be done, even though it means that hands and feet are to be nailed to the Cross!"

Jesus in His life and death and in His Agony gave to God the Father in loving obedience all the knowledge, all the reverence, and all the service possible in the use of God's creation. Most of all did He fulfil the will of the Creator in obeying the precepts of God. Jesus observed all the Commandments perfectly. To the one true God He offered sacrifice, and sanctified His Name. That sacrifice has never ceased to make holy every Sabbath. Jesus honored His Heavenly Father, and in His death made lasting His honor to His earthly Mother.

Jesus was slain that man might live, and His pure body was exposed to shame and pain to purify your pleasures. Jesus restored to you the inheritance stolen from you by the disobedience of Adam. Jesus bore witness in favor even of His slayers, and in His Heart was no covetousness of person or thing but the desire that all should obey the will of the Father in His Commandments and say with Him, "Thy will be done!"

Fiat of Redemption

FIAT. The second great fiat is the Fiat of the Redemption; and the first scene of the closing act in that sublime drama is made manifest to you in the Agony of the Garden through the suffering of the leading character, Jesus, the Redeemer. "Let man be saved!" is His Fiat; and man is saved.

That salvation is measured out generously. One grief, one pang would have been sufficient in its infinite merit to satisfy God's justice; but Jesus sorrowed and was wracked in every way for you. He may be said to have endured a thousand deaths. He might have dismissed the tortures of the morrow from His mind and have lifted His soul to Paradise, but He deliberately fastened His attention upon His Passion and bore it all even in anticipation.

The measure which Jesus set for your mercy to others, He has kept in His mercy to you. "Forgive, and you shall be forgiven. Give, and it shall be given to you; good measure and pressed down and shaken together and running over shall they give into your bosom."

The obedience of Jesus in His Agony was not only the obedience of law; it was the obedience of love also. Jesus fulfilled the counsels that He gave us, as well as the Commandments which God gave us. "If you will," He says, "follow Me. I do not command; I lead, that you, generous heart, may have the courage and ardor to leave all." If the followers of Jesus left their treasures and possessions, so did He. If they left friends and kindred, so did He. If they left home and country, so did He.

To do the will of the Father, Jesus left His own Mother desolate in the Temple and is to leave her on the morrow heart-broken at the foot of the Cross. Thousands of martyrs have left life itself with Jesus, in loving obedience to His counsels. Fiat, fiat! Let the Commandments of the Father be fulfilled! Let the counsels of the Son be followed! Let it be done!

Fiat of Sanctification

FIAT. The third Divine fiat is the Fiat of Sanctification, the Fiat of the Third Person of the Trinity, of the Holy Spirit. "This is the will of God," says St. Paul, "your sanctification." Jesus in His Agony fulfilled all precepts and all counsels; and more than that, He fulfilled them perfectly. "Be ye perfect, as your Heavenly Father is perfect," was a counsel of Jesus which He followed to the letter.

Jesus was the ideal ever before His followers in their pursuit of perfection. If the darkness loomed before them, they thought of the black gloom of the Passion. If their feet were heavy or wounded, they were treading in footprints reddened with the blood of their Leader. Their hearts might be constrained with dread apprehension, but they knew that they were not crushed by such a vise as wrung the life-blood from the Heart of Jesus.

With the coming of the Holy Spirit the followers of Jesus were transformed. The tongues of fire that flamed upon Apostles and disciples were reflected in their eyes and glistened upon their lips, and spoke in every zealous act as well as in every burning word. They were no longer heavy with sleep. They were not runaways any more; no, they faced with joy their persecutors.

Could they not watch one hour? Assuredly; and for a whole life through they will watch with sleepless eyes, obedient with their Leader even to the death of the Cross. You are to have their ideals; you are to equal their performance; you are to attain to their perfection. The Holy Spirit whispers His Fiat to your souls, and you answer: "Fiat; let it be done!"

You have Mary as your model. In the Annunciation she echoed for us all her Fiat, "Be it done to me according to Thy word." God made your redemption and your sanctification dependent upon our Blessed Lady's consent, and though a sword was to pierce her soul, she cried: "Thy will be done!" She too lived and said the "Our Father," and she is with you as you watch the hour with Jesus in agony.

Prayer

Father, Son, and Holy Spirit, You who have willed our creation, our redemption, and our sanctification, aid our weak wills with the strengthening power of grace, that we may persevere to life eternal in the perfect fulfillment of the Divine will. *Amen.*

THY WILL BE DONE

Thou hast sown the skies with splendor;
Thou hast flushed with gold the sun;
Yet can I love's pauper, tender
Purer gold through Thy will done.

O Lord Almighty, who permittest evil to draw good therefrom, hear our humble prayers, and grant that we remain faithful to Thee unto death. Grant us also, through the intercession of most holy Mary, the strength ever to conform ourselves to Thy most holy Will.

"*My God, unite all minds in the truth and all hearts in charity!*"

"*O Jesus Christ, Son of the living God, Light of the world, I adore Thee, for Thee I live, for Thee I die. Amen.*"

May the most just, most high and most adorable will of God be in all things done, praised and magnified forever!"

Thy Will Be Done
On Earth As It Is In Heaven

Fiat Voluntas Tua Sicut In Coelo Et In Terra

The Ideal

VOLUNTAS TUA. The fulfillment of God's will is the ideal that is to be realized by all creation; in justice, if it needs be, but in love assuredly. Jesus in His life sets before you the perfect realization of that ideal. In the head of the book it is written of Me that I should do Thy will, O God," say the Psalmist and St. Paul about our Lord.

God's will led Jesus to take the body of our slavery, to be born in poverty, to be lost to His Mother, to bury Himself in Nazareth, to leave home and be baptized. "My meat," He says, "is to do the will of Him that sent Me." The will of God makes the family of Jesus as well as His food. "Whosoever shall do the will of My Father, that is in Heaven, he is My brother and sister and mother."

Jesus in His Passion realizes in a still more perfect form the will of the Father. Jesus longed for His baptism of blood; but that you might know there was intense pain accompanying His intense desire, He revealed to you the bitterness of His chalice, a foretaste of the acrid cup of His Crucifixion. "Father, if it be possible, let this chalice pass from Me; but yet not My will, but Thine be done."

And then Jesus sealed for you that compact with the red seal of His blood. "Think diligently upon Him that endured such opposition from sinners against Himself, that you be not wearied, fainting in your minds. For you have not yet resisted unto blood, striving against sin."

Jesus may not ask of you the supreme test of martyrdom. If He does, He will give you strength to go to death rejoicing. Jesus, however, does ask of you gratitude. "In all things give thanks; for this is the will of God in Christ Jesus concerning you all." You are thanking God by this hour of prayer, while you watch with Jesus in His agony. You make grateful reparation for the many who ignore or even oppose the will of God.

You do not take the gifts of God in indifference and as a matter of course. The widespread sunlight, the free airs of Heaven, the abundant waters of the earth, your faith, your sorrow for sin, your progress in virtue are for you blessings that come to you from wounded hands. You see in everything the pierced Heart of Jesus which sanctifies you and all creation.

The Ideal Realized

SICUT IN COELO. The ideal fulfillment of God's will on earth finds its complete realization in Heaven. St. Paul has put the truth briefly and fully: "Having joy set before Him, Jesus endured the Cross, despising the shame, and now sits at the right hand of God." You may look beyond the shadows of the Garden of Gethsemane and see the joyous dawn of Easter and of eternity from which Christ Jesus turned away His eyes. Now He sits at the right hand of God.

That throne shall be for you and for all who say in their hearts and fulfill in life "Thy will be done as in Heaven." You see now in Heaven every wound a star, every drop of blood converted into a refreshing dew, every shadow transfused to sunlight, every throb of pain become a thrill of joy. The Tabor which Jesus denied Himself in His Agony is His eternally, realizing forever in transfiguring glory the ideal which He lived and followed even unto the death of the Cross.

If the ideal of God's will is realized in a glorified body, much more is God's will realized in a glorified soul. Your wayward thoughts are shepherded to a Heavenly fold because your Good Shepherd sought you through the poignant search of His Agony. Your sinful desires and the evil wishes of the world have through the atonement of Jesus and by the repentance of the offender been changed in Heaven into ardent rays of purest love centering upon God.

The tortured thoughts of your Saviour have triumphed. The weight of mankind's sinfulness, which crushed from His veins the wine of His Blood, is in Heaven lifted from all souls. No stain of sin remains now on the souls which have been laved to whiteness. The hour of Agony in the Garden is the promise and pledge of God's will fulfilled for the blessed in the unending hours of Heaven.

The Real Idealized

ET IN TERRA. To have the ideal realized the real must be idealized. The thoughts of Christ Jesus in His Agony must be your thoughts. "Be not conformed to this world," cries St. Paul; "but be reformed in the newness of your mind, that you may prove what is the good, and the acceptable, and the perfect will of God."

To have that new form fashioned out of new thoughts, you must have within you the mind of Jesus. As His life began and ended with an offering of all to the will of God, so for you every sunlight and every starlight must realize on earth, as far as sincere wish can effect, the Heavenly ideal. Christian principles shall be your principles.

So too shall Christ's resolution be yours, to raise the real to the ideal. A right mind, if followed by a right will, will give you the possession above all earthly possessions — a Christian character. The gratitude of act surpasses the gratitude of word or thought.

Imitation is sincerest flattery, and imitation of Jesus is your finest way of repairing for the ingratitude of man. The soldier who reproduces the courage of his captain, the student who is as studious as his teacher, the child who gives back to parents in deed some of their sacrificing devotion—they are all truly grateful. Jesus is your Captain, your Schoolmaster, your Parent to eternal life; and in Gethsemane He is all that and more.

Let, then, that will be in you which was in Christ Jesus.

You will realize to the full the will of God, which has its ideal in Heaven, if you have within you, together with His thoughts and His will, the heart also of Jesus.

Jesus for you put His whole Heart into everything He did. His Heart sent forth its currents in a thousand jets in His Agony, and opened Itself wide upon the Cross to give the truest testimony of His devotion to God's will, Jesus inspired the opened treasures of the Magi. He opened in the widest embrace His arms upon the Cross and died with an opened Heart. Those gashed lips upon His heart bespeak His generous love and demand your grateful return of love. "Thou wouldst not," said Jesus to ungrateful Jerusalem when He would gather her children under His opened wings. If Jerusalem would not, you will.

The Catholic poet Dante pictured the Angels of God as forming themselves into an immense eagle hovering over the heights of Heaven. The real wings outspread there are the wings of God's mercy, expanded to the widest and enfolding beneath them all the blessed, whom the agonizing Jesus saved to celebrate forever the will of God.

Prayer

Perfect Exemplar of God's will, Jesus, our suffering Saviour, give to us a mind and a heart like Thine, that the willing accord of the blessed in Heaven may find a grateful echo in all the souls of earth. *Amen*.

ON EARTH AS IT IS IN HEAVEN

May the barren wastes grow flowered
May drab dross have golden worth?

Yes, weak prayer divinely dowered
Makes a Heaven of our earth.

>–·◆·–○–·◆·–◄

O Lord, who in the mystery of the glorious Transfiguration of Thy Divine Son, didst deign to make resplendent the truth of the holy Catholic Faith, and to confirm miraculously, by Thy very word, spoken from a cloud, our perfect adoption as Thy sons; we humbly beg of Thee to grant that we may in truth become coheirs of this same King of Glory, and share in Thy everlasting happiness. Amen.

"Divine Heart of Jesus, convert sinners, save the dying, set free the holy souls in Purgatory!"

"O Lord Jesus, most merciful Saviour of the world, we beg and beseech Thee through Thy most Sacred Heart that all wandering sheep may now return to Thee, the shepherd and Bishop of their souls, who livest etc."

Give Us This Day
Da Nobis Hodie

Private Prayer

DA. "Give" is the word consecrated to prayer. In various forms the word is found in every prayer of the Church. Petition, it is true, is not the only purpose of prayer; but it is the most usual purpose. In the Garden of Olivet Jesus made petition to the Father. As during His life, so now in His preparation for death He becomes a model for you and a standard for you in private prayer. In the "Our Father" which Jesus taught you, after addressing God and asking reverence for His name and advent for His Kingdom and fulfillment of His will, then you are told to make petition for yourself and say "Our Father, who art in Heaven, give to us."

Jesus was always at prayer. His every act and thought and slightest wish was a prayer to His Father for you. The mother who cares for her sick child may not utter aloud her pitiful desire, but you may detect her pleading to God in her every look and in every touch that she gives to her ailing one. Her whole day, distracted though it may be with manifold duties, is centered upon that bed of sickness. Her heart is there, no matter where her thoughts may turn. The anxious mother is but a faint image of your Saviour, whose Heart in toil, in suffering, in death, was lovingly intent upon you and upon all sinners, apart from prayer as well as now in His agonizing prayer.

Intention is more important in prayer than attention, and that is why by your Morning Offering you put into every thought, work, and suffering a tongue of prayer, as Jesus did in His life. Yet, though the love of the heart can pierce with its rays all distractions, attention must help to insure intention and make it more intense and more ardent.

Jesus in all His private prayer, as now in the Garden of Olives, safeguards attention. He goes apart, as He did so often before, into the darkness of the night, far from the noise and turmoil of men. He shuts out the world before He kneels and brings in Heaven. He gives to His prayer an attentive body and attentive senses, as well as a loving Heart intent upon God.

Public Prayer

OBIS. Jesus practised public prayer also. On great occasions He resorted to prayer: at the tomb of Lazarus, before choosing His Apostles, when about to appoint Peter to the Primacy, on Mount Tabor, and in the great prayer at the Last Supper. The Our Father is placed by the Church at a most solemn and prominent position in the middle of the Canon of the Mass, between Consecration and Communion. The "Our Father" is in form a public prayer. "Give us," we beg; not "Give me."

You know that every prayer, while a petition for grace, is also a means of grace. Prayer is a sacramental of the Church, and like other religious acts has the power to merit remission of venial sins, merit grace, and increase sanctity in the soul. It is the prayer of Jesus and His Atonement which converts the dross of your human prayer into the precious gold that shall ever be sovereign currency in Heaven.

The Sacraments of the Church are also public prayers, which, like the sacramentals, have through the sorrow and pain of Jesus become the healing and solace of all mankind. Recall the Sacraments that have come into your life and into the lives of your friends, and you will remember that these fountains of grace were opened by the Redeemer. In His Agony Jesus laments that many fail to drink of these fountains. He may, however, permit Himself some comfort in the vision of the countless souls who have partaken of the waters springing up to eternal life.

The greatest public prayer of the Church, the Mass, is closely associated with the hour of Jesus in Gethsemane. The Precious Blood was shed mystically at the Last Supper, when the changed substance of the Wine was set apart from the consecrated Bread. Who shall say how often you have seen the priest at the altar bowing over the bread and wine before he hallows them as Minister of Christ. Look now at Jesus bowed in the Garden, while the wine of sacrifice reddens the raiment of His Body.

Persevering Prayer

BODIE. Your prayer must be today, and that means every day and always. You are to talk in prayer and to walk in prayer and to think in prayer. Yes, and your every heart-beat should accompany the heart-beat of Jesus and repeat, "Give us this day! Give us this day!" In persevering prayer Jesus offers to you a splendid and encouraging example. "Being in agony, He prayed the longer," St. Luke tells you. Jesus persevered in prayer despite the weariness of His Body and despite the depressing weight that His foreshadowed Passion put upon senses and nerves. May you never have the anguish of body which hardly permits you to whisper your prayer! Should such a time come, and you can only express your desires by the silent messengers of shed blood, you will be strengthened by your fellow sufferer, Jesus, who prayed the longer in His Agony and let His sweat of blood speak to God for Him.

Persevere, too, in prayer against the heavier weariness of mind. "My soul," said Jesus in Gethsemane, "is sorrowful unto death." The tortures of the morrow were already present to His thoughts. The cry of the misguided mob, "Crucify Him," horrifying as it was, made but slight sound beside the hideous din of the world's sinfulness clamoring through all time for the Crucifixion of Jesus. You can form no idea of the anguished mind of Jesus. He alone, as God, understood the heinousness of sin. The mind of Jesus feels your affronts more than you do, because they are sins against the Father and against Him. The sin that wounds you pierced through His Heart before it reached you; yet, with all that agony, Jesus did but pray the longer.

Persevere, lastly, against weariness of will. To give love and receive hatred in return—that wearies the will of Jesus. To see millions of men ignoring God or offending Him and neglectful of all prayer, is likely to make you tepid. Fervor is the youth of good will, and tepidity, which is sloth of soul, is the old age of the will. The wings of prayer can scarcely lift aloft the tepid soul. Then, slothful will, you must stand by the side of Jesus. Carry on with Him. He rallied from the crushing weight of the Agony. He rose beneath the increasing load of the Cross and staggered to His death. "Not My will but Thine be done," is the assurance to all that the will of Jesus is persevering in prayer, and unfailing pledge that you too can persevere with Him in prayer.

Prayer

Jesus, model of persevering prayer, grant us through the manifold graces of Thy Agony that with attention of body and intention of soul we may not grow faint in our agonies, but with Thee pray ever the longer. *Amen.*

Our Father Hymn

Father of all, high or lowly,
We, Thy children, voice our prayer:
May Thy name be held most holy,
Hallowed ever everywhere!

May Thy Kingdom find hearts willing,
Throning Thee in loyal love!
May Thy will have glad fulfilling
Here as in Thy realm above!

Give us bread that daily better
For Thy love we all may live;
And as we forgive each debtor
So do Thou our debts forgive!

When sin tempts, we pray Thee guide us
Making sure our victory:
Stay, Our Father, stay beside us
And from evil set us free!

AIR: ANY *Tantum Ergo* MELODY

Wonderful is the Name of God.

"O Jesus in the most holy Sacrament, have mercy on us!"

"O Jesus Christ, Son of the living God. Light of the World, I adore Thee; for Thee I live; for Thee I die. Amen."

"O Jesus, life eternal in the bosom of the Father, life of souls created in Thy likeness, in the name of Thy love, make known and reveal Thy Heart!"

Our Daily Bread
Panem Nostrum Quotidianum

Bread of Body

PANEM. The first petition for ourselves that we make to our Father is for bread. Bread is the food of life, and it signifies for us life and all the necessities of life. The fallen race of man was doomed to eat its bread in the sweat of its brow. The labor that was a curse, Jesus changed into a blessing for you and for all. He won for you eternal life by the sweat of His Blood. Every bead of your sweat has by the suffering and death of Jesus been converted into a pearl of great price purchasing Heaven.

You should, then, even if you had all the ills of Job to put up with, persevere in patience and hope. The gate to the Garden of Gethsemane opened for sorrow to Jesus, but for gladness to you. You have a hope that Job did not have. Jesus has made your sufferings a means of sanctity, a merit of higher place in Heaven, a prayer and satisfaction for others. Your fastings, your pains are bread of

Heavenly life to others as well as to yourself. Your tiny agonies, your little crucifixions are made Divine by the Divinity of Jesus.

Even if your prayer for life and its necessities is not answered as a short-sighted hope might demand; even if you fast instead of feeding abundantly; still, our Father is answering your prayer. Jesus brought life out of death. The Father left the body of Jesus without food during His Passion, when hosts of Angels might have brought Him sustenance and comfort, when the heavens could have sent down manna. God is not short-sighted. Human hope must change to Divine hope; as you enter upon your passion, and Divine hope assures you that the Father is giving you better bread when He is withholding what you ask for.

Bread of Soul

NOSTRUM. Our bread is not the bread of the body only; it is also the bread of the soul. The wicked, in Proverbs, are said to eat the bread of wickedness and to drink the wine of iniquity.

Increase your faith and you increase your hope. "Faith is the substance of things to be hoped for," St. Paul tells you. Behind the food is the hand of the Giver, but it calls for greater faith to see behind the fasting the hand of the Withdrawer. Every book you read to illuminate and strengthen your faith, every word you hear which gives courage and endurance to your good resolutions, every secret prayer and good wish of your heart — that is the daily bread of your soul.

Enter Gethsemane without faith, and you behold a stricken man, who knows that his enemies are closing in upon him and that he is to be hurried to an ignominious death by fomented rioting and by a weak official. Look out on your life, on the history of the Church, the state of the world, and without faith everything is confused and disheartening.

Now look at both scenes with the eyes of faith. The man of Gethsemane is God. His human weakness is Divine strength. The plotting of the enemies of Jesus, the wild frenzy of the mob, the faltering compromises of Pilate, the power of Jerusalem and the tyranny of Rome, are all characters in a tragic drama which is composed and is directed to a thrice-happy ending by an infinitely masterful mind. The darkness of Gethsemane is made lightsome by faith; its roughness is an even road; its barren lot is golden with wheat; and out of its stones Jesus has made for you the Bread of Life.

Read the history of the Church and of the world with the blinded vision of human reason, and you are disheartened. Violence, confusion, wars, pestilence, rampant evils torment the aching sight. All seem shreds and tags and tattered fragments, presenting an intricate, unintelligible puzzle. Not so to the eyes of faith; not so to you who know that it is Jesus who began the last stage of His work, to be consummated on the Cross. For you and to faith the world's history is a tapestry of glorious design, planned and brought to completion by God, the Divine Weaver, of which you see only the reverse side.

Bread of the Altar

QUOTIDIANUM. When Jesus taught you the "Our Father" and told you to ask for your daily bread, He surely did not forget the Heavenly Bread of the Altar which He bade us to partake of. That is the Bread which makes us all of one family. "We, being many," says St. Paul, "are one bread, one body, all that partake of one bread."

The Bread of the Altar has always been looked upon as the bond of charity. You love God because you see Him in the universe in which He is present. You love your neighbors because you see in them the image of God. Jesus in His Bread devised another Divine Presence, to increase our love of God and to unite us in ties of family love with all our fellow men.

God is powerful in His world, giving it activity and supporting its activity. Write your name in steel, in marble, in sand, in water, in air, and the weaker the material the stronger must be the power to keep your name in existence. "You are the letters of Christ," says St. Paul. You have been fashioned out of nothing, and you need Omnipotence to perpetuate your existence. Through the Bread of the Altar Jesus exercises a conserving power on the letters which He wrote upon the fleshy tablets of your heart. The sign of His Baptism is there, and it is indelible. The signs of His grace are there, and are kept intact by the Food which Jesus gives to you daily.

God's perfections are found in His world, together with His presence and power. Creation bears the vestiges of God, and gives in faint shadows His Divine excellences. In his spiritual soul, in his personality, in his ability to know and to love, man is an image of God. "God is love," as St. John tells us, and charity in man is the image of that love. You have in the Bread of the Altar an evidence of charity indicative of supreme love. Love seeks union, and Jesus, becoming your food, incorporates Himself into your body while by grace He perfects the likeness to God in your soul.

Jesus dipped bread into wine at the Last Supper and gave the food to His betrayer, in a last appeal of hospitality and love to win back His sinful Apostle from treachery. For you Jesus went into Gethsemane and dipped His sacred Body into the Blood of His Passion. The Bread of the Altar comes to you with the wine of Christ's Blood, strengthening you against all betrayal and increasing in you friendship for Him. Nowhere are the presence, power, and perfections of God more signally manifested than in the Bread of the Altar, made of grain that was harvested in sorrow, milled in crushing pain, and permeated with atoning Blood.

Prayer

God of goodness, Source of our life, who hast by Thy gracious presence and supreme perfections made manifest Thy love in all things and in all men, increase our faith and our hope and most of all our charity, that we may daily partake of the Bread of Divine love together with Thy children and our brethren, and that we may be one with them unto life eternal. *Amen.*

GIVE US OUR DAILY BREAD

Not the miracle of manna;
That might idle hands abet,

Dole us for our hearts' hosanna
Bread bedewed with beads of sweat!

><+>•O•<+><

Thou art the Christ, the Son of the living God.

"*Eucharistic Heart of Jesus, have mercy on us!*"

"*Most sweet Jesus, increase my faith, hope and charity and give me a humble, contrite heart!*"

"*Let us with Mary Immaculate adore, thank, pray to and console the most sacred and well-beloved Eucharistic Heart of Jesus!*"

Forgive Us Our Trespasses
Dimitte Nobis Debita Nostra

God and Sin

DEBITA. "Father, forgive them; they know not what they do." Those who crucified Jesus surely did not know what they were doing. But do you or does anyone know the malice of sin? Does not Jesus say to you out of the sorrow and gloom of the Garden what He said to the Father from His Cross? "You do not know what you do." You do know that an offense against a stranger is not rated by you as great as an offense against an acquaintance. Now if the acquaintance is a friend, and the friend a relative, and the relative a brother, a father, a mother, you and the whole world consider that the closer the connection, the greater will be the offense. Think, then, of the intimate closeness and the actual presence of God in every sin. Freedom of will gives to you the terrible power of making God cooperate in the action of sin though not in the sinfulness of the act.

"Father, forgive them; they know not what they do." Who fully realizes the fact that the higher the dignity of the person offended, the more malicious is the offense? To beat a horse is cruel and inhuman; to beat an innocent child is barbarous; to insult and maltreat the great men to whom all give well deserved honor, is an act of callous brutality; to slay a wise and generous ruler is the sin of regicide, shocking to everyone except blind fanatics. Estimate then what it means to offend God. The monstrous crime of deicide committed on the innocent, wise and kind-hearted Redeemer fills you with disgust and horror. And yet do you not know that in a sense every sin is deicidal. Sin made a target of Jesus in His Agony and Passion, and it makes a target of God. Its malice is so heinous and deadly that were it possible it would slay God.

Unite now the nearness of offender and offended with the high excellence of the Person of God to whom the offense is offered, and though you shall never know what you do when you sin, you will know better what Jesus suffered for you in the Garden of Olives. Jesus took upon Himself the sins of mankind. Who could be closer to God the Father than the Son of God, one in nature with the Father and united to Him in Person through the Holy Spirit, the God of Love? Who knew and appreciated to the full the excellence of God better than Jesus, joining to His Divine Person human and divine natures? The Heart of Jesus visioning the sins of the world turned in loathing from the sight, and every drop of His sinless Blood fled horror-stricken to escape the deadly plague of sin.

Man-God and Sin

NOSTRA. You pray in the Our Father that the debts owed to divine justice be remitted for all mankind as well as for yourself. The hideous horde of sin which rushed from the four corners of the world upon Jesus in Agony is past numbering except by the infinite wisdom of God. You might form some idea of the abominations which overwhelmed the sensitive innocence of Jesus, if you had before you, as Jesus had, the transcendent vision of original justice, as planned by God for man. The mutilations of war are made more heart-rending in a soldier when the splendid perfections of his former manhood are remembered. Jesus knew the glory of original justice, and He shuddered, and His soul was sorrowful even to death at the devastating ravages made by original sin.

Yet, after all, original sin is not actual sin, and the spectacle of its loss was not as harrowing to Jesus as that of the countless lesser offenses which are called venial sins. The services and sacramentals of the Church, the aspirations and prayers, the very Our Father which you are trying to understand during this hour, all through the saving grace of Jesus remove completely the unnumbered particles of blackening dust which by venial faults daily burden the souls of men. Thanks to Jesus and His Passion you are daily cleansed of such daily stains. You may not forget, however, that upon His snow-white soul Jesus saw all the venial sins of man come raining down, as from the clouds of an erupting volcano destroying ashes encrust fields of flowers or grain.

You will find it hard to understand the words of St. Paul that Jesus knew no sin and yet was "made sin for us that we might be made in Him the justice of God." How sinlessness is made sin will become clearer in Heaven, but of this you may be sure, Jesus experienced the horrors of sin without having the guilt of the slightest fault. You know that beside original sin and venial sin the more heinous malice of mortal sin visited Jesus in the way God's justice demanded, and the willing love of the Redeemer accepted the visitation. Imagine, then, the sins of all the race of man from creation to the end of time, marshalling themselves in serried ranks and trampling into blood and slime their stainless Victim. Group, if you will, the armies of guilt under the standards of the seven deadly sins, study those sins in the history of man, note them at work in Christ's Passion, and if the vastness of the havoc appalls you, the glorious victory of Jesus will console and comfort you.

Man and Sin

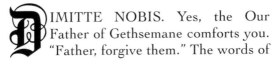IMITTE NOBIS. Yes, the Our Father of Gethsemane comforts you. "Father, forgive them." The words of

Jesus are a sacrament as well as a prayer. They ask, and they perform what they ask. Jesus was claiming His due. "If I shall be lifted up, I will draw all to me." The malice of sin attacking the infinite excellence of God incurred infinite guilt. Only God could offer adequate atonement, and man it was who must offer atonement. The happy union was brought about, "Mercy and truth have met each other; justice and peace have kissed. Truth is sprung out of the earth and justice has looked down from Heaven." That divine espousal was consummated in the Passion and Agony of Jesus, and from Jesus the God-man came our all merciful and all just Redemption.

Forgiveness which comes from the heart is most consoling, and Jesus has put in rubrics that all can read the message of God's loving forgiveness. No better attestation of full forgiveness could you ask for. Your likeness to God which was disfigured by sin is restored and ennobled. The justice of the Redemption repairs the ravages of original sin and builds a grander edifice upon the ruin of Adam. "Happy fault," the Church dares to say, "which merited so excellent a Redeemer." God, who must keep sin at limitless distance from Him, is present in the souls of men through the powerful attraction of grace.

Jesus has prayed and has fasted for you, and shed tears of blood for you. He has given you a picture of Himself in the parable of the Prodigal's father. Forgiveness for Jesus means joy in Heaven and joy upon earth. Jesus through forgiveness and grace not only brings God to your soul, not only makes you partakers of divinity, not only gives you Heaven as your inheritance, but He also makes you a child of God and clothes you in the finest raiment and sets you beside Him at the banquet of eternity. "This my son who was dead, is come to life." Yes, my God and my Savior. I am forgiven and have life again through Thy Agony and through Thy death.

Prayer

God of all holiness who hast in the Incarnation of Thy Son united justice with mercy, forgive Thy erring children and let them see, as Jesus saw, the infinite horror of sin and by the help of His Passion vest their souls with the grace of persevering sanctity. *Amen.*

FORGIVE US

Nailed with Christ give benediction;
Hush your lip's revengeful cries;

Angered heart, that crucifixion
Shall to-day win Paradise.

><|><-O-><|><

Into Thy hands, O Lord, and the hands of the Angels, I place and entrust this day my own soul, my relations, my benefactors, my friends and enemies, and all Catholic people; keep us during this day, by the merits and intercession of the Blessed Virgin Mary and all the Saints, from the vices, evil desires, sins, and temptations of the Evil One, from sudden and unprovided death, and from the pains of Hell. May the light of the Holy Spirit and Thy grace shine in my heart. Let me ever obey Thy commandments, and let me never be separated from Thee, who as God livest and reignest with the Father and the Holy Spirit for ever and ever. Amen.

"Sacred Heart of Jesus, I trust in Thee." "Sweet Jesus, be to me not a judge but a Saviour!"

"Eternal Father, I offer Thee the Precious Blood of Jesus Christ in satisfaction for my sins and for the wants of Holy Church."

As We Forgive Those Who Trespass Against Us

Sicut Et Nos Dimittimus Debitoribus Nostris

Jesus Preaches Forgiveness

SICUT. When Jesus taught you to pray for your forgiveness by means of the Our Father, He put into prayer and for the love of your heart one of the virtues dearest to His Heart. Much of the Old Testament Jesus fulfilled and made more perfect, but one practice of the Old Law He annulled and abolished, the barbarous and inhuman practice of an eye for an eye. Reprisals may satisfy for the moment the savage craving for revenge that lowers man to the level of the brute. Reprisals, however, are foolish and futile; they invite further reprisals until vendettas stain the years with blood-shed and exterminate whole families.

Jesus who bade you turn the other cheek rather than strike back, would have you offer the other eye rather than blind your enemy.

"I wish mercy and not sacrifice," said Jesus, and He filled His life with mercy, mercy for the hungering, mercy for the sick and suffering, mercy for His calumniators and persecutors. Patience and forgiveness heal wounds and promote lasting peace. The flesh that is constantly irritated, is likely to become cancerous. So, when Jesus tells you to add to your petition for forgiveness, the condition, "As we forgive," He wishes you to dismiss wholly from your heart any irritating and persistent longing for revenge, lest the wound fester the soul with the ugly cancer of death.

"Put up thy sword," said Jesus to impulsive Peter, healing the wounded servant. Jesus does not want from you the sharp edge of the sword; He wants from you the healing touch of mercy. The prayer in the Agony of the Garden was surely a prayer of mercy. Jesus asks for no reprisals or revenge. He presents both cheeks to His foes, to be struck, yes, and His whole body to be lacerated. He does not seek death for death, but to His murderers He grants, if they will have it, eternal life.

Jesus Practices Forgiveness

ET NOS. When you say the Our Father, you should, in order to express the sense fully, put the stress of your voice on "we". In the Latin the emphasis is clearly expressed and might be rendered, "Just as we ourselves forgive." Why is the thought so expressed? Because your forgiveness of others is a condition to your own forgiveness. Listen to Jesus, "If you forgive men their offenses, your heavenly Father will forgive you also your offenses. But if you will not forgive men, neither will your Father forgive you your offenses." Jesus will hold you to your promise. Did He not picture for you in the parable of the wicked servant what happens to those who do not fulfill the condition which they daily repeat in the Our Father. "Thou wicked servant" says the Master; "I forgave thee all the debt because thou hadst besought me; shouldst not thou then have had compassion also on thy fellow-servant as I had compassion on thee?"

If the words, "As we forgive" are a condition, they are also a comparison. "Forgive us, Father, just as we ourselves forgive." Happily for you the Father is more generous in forgiveness to you than you can possibly be to others. You know well that if the offense committed against you was a willful and deliberate offense, then it was a greater insult and injustice to God than to you. You grieve for the harm done to you; Jesus feels that very harm more intensely than you, because He feels your injustice and the injustice to God which you often forget in the heat of your own grievance. Consider, too, that your slightest offense against God is felt by Jesus more keenly than any possible offense of man to you. Yet God forgives you and Jesus suffers for the offenses of you and of your enemy.

The grievous burden, alas, of our offenses weighs Jesus to the ground in His Agony. When you kneel beside Him and say with Him the Our Father, you will assuredly at the height of His sufferings, rid yourself of all resentment and put into your heart the loving forgiveness of Jesus. "I have left all my grievances," you will tell Him, outside the Garden of Olives. Jesus, the sinless One, who never trespassed

against God or man, deigns to repute Himself
a sinner and prays with you, "Forgive us as we
forgive." At the side of the great and merciful Heart of Jesus, there is no place for the
spiteful meanness of revenge. You generously
accept the condition and you practice forgiveness as Jesus practices forgiveness.

Jesus Perfects Forgiveness

DIMITTIMUS DEBITORIBUS NOS-
TRIS. It is no cold, no reluctant, no
partial forgiveness that Jesus pro-
poses to you. By your forgiveness you are to
prove to the world that you are Christians:
"By this shall all men know you, that you
have love one for another." You are not to
postpone forgiveness. As Jesus forgave you
before the sun went down on Calvary, so you
too must not let the sun go down on your
anger. When you lay your gift upon God's
altar and remember your fault, you must has-
ten to be reconciled. Your gifts to God should
be as full of merciful forgiveness as the gift
to God which Jesus laid for you on the
Altar of the Cross. And how often shall you

forgive? Will it be as often as you have offended others or others have offended you; will it be as often as you have offended God? It will be more often still. You shall forgive seventy times seven times, and that is more often than always.

Note that this high standard of forgiveness was attained by Jesus. He confounded the accusers of the woman taken in sin, and they departed, saying to themselves, "Do not stone us sinners as we do not stone others." Jesus did not rebuff the apostle who doubted when all believed. "Bring hither," He said to Thomas, "thy hand and put it into my side." The public sinner was permitted to touch Him and do Him kind services. The only rebuke given to Peter was a reproachful glance, and he who denied Jesus thrice, was kindly permitted to give triple profession of his love.

What finally is the forgiveness which Jesus is perfecting for you in His Agony? His basest offender, the one who had been the trusted apostle, the one who a short time before sat at the table of the Savior, Judas, the betrayer, was not struck down by the sword, was not crushed by hosts of summoned angels, but was welcomed as a friend. The sweat of His Blood was still upon the lips of Jesus when He kissed the traitor in reproachful forgiveness. May Jesus not address that reproach to you; may He not feel that you too have sold Him to be crucified for the paltry price of hatred and revenge! Forgive us our trespasses just as we forgive those who trespass against us.

Prayer

Merciful and loving Jesus, who hast not willed the death of the sinner but that he be converted and live, give to us all a heart of perfect forgiveness that as we are to be united in one family in Heaven, so we may, as Thy children, love one another upon earth. *Amen.*

AS WE FORGIVE

Brother, harm not erring brother.
Though with snow-white hands you stone;

You who stoop to smite another,
Pelt with death the Sinless One.

O Holy Spirit, sweet guest of my soul, remain with me, and see that I ever remain with Thee.

"*O Lord, preserve the faith in us!*"

"*Jesus, meek and humble of heart, make my heart like to Thine!*"

"*Sweet Heart of my Jesus, make me love Thee ever more and more!*"

And Lead Us Not Into Temptation

Et Ne Nos Inducas In Tentationem

Our Weakness

ET NE NOS. Sin the real evil and only true evil is the subject of the fifth petition in the Our Father. In the sixth petition you pray with Jesus in His Agony that you may be made safe against any temptation which might lead you to sin. Jesus in Gethsemane foresaw the trials which were shortly to come upon His Apostles and He exhorted them earnestly to prepare. Who can doubt that He was thinking of the Our Father when He said, "Watch ye and pray lest you enter into temptation. The spirit indeed is willing but the flesh is weak." Truly the flesh is weak, and it was the will of Jesus to let us witness that weakness of body in His Agony. He moves restlessly back and forth. He makes a pitiful appeal, "What, could you not watch one hour with Me?" He gave sad expression to His excessive weariness, and that you might have the evidence of your own eyes, He let His Body be bathed in a sweat of blood. Contrast all that with the calmness, silence and dignity of Jesus throughout His life and through the rest of the Passion. Then you will understand that this weakness of His Body was meant to give your body strength in the hour of temptation.

You need strength of mind also against the assaults of temptation. You must keep your faith ardent and your principles shiningly clear, as you move about in a world cold to the example of Jesus, in a world which ignores or despises the truths which Jesus taught. It is a test to your faith to see thousands denying that faith in word and in act. Pray that your mind be made strong if temptations against your faith or your virtue assail you. Fill your mind with good reading which will clarify and confirm for you the truths of faith. Your imagination through ear and eye, through books and pictures is haunted with scenes of vice. Put before your mind's eye the lives of God's saints, and the inspiring spectacle of Jesus in His Agony. His Soul is sorrowful even to death that by His merits and by His example your spirit may be resolute always in right thinking and in right living.

Most of all for your weakness you must watch and pray that your irresolute will may not be overcome by temptation. In the free will and there alone is the battle lost when you are tempted. Your bodily weariness and pain, your distracted and unenlightened mind may be such as to preclude any rational act and so any sin, but when your will knowingly and deliberately consents, then you have surrendered to the enemy. Jesus permits you to look into the fierce battle of the will, when He cried out, "Father, if it be possible, let this chalice pass from me." Then He permits you to witness the victory of His unconquered will, when He continued, But not my will but Thine be done." Jesus displays the numberless wounds of His struggle when He sheds His Blood at every pore. Jesus assures you of His complete triumph when being in agony, He prays the longer.

Our Watchfulness

CONDUCAS. You have unhappy experience of your weakness of body, mind and will, and so you are fully aware that you must not expose yourself to the occasions of sin. When you are convalescing from an illness, how careful you are to be properly protected from inclement weather, how solicitous your friends are that through exposure you suffer no relapse. Now your weakened soul and body after the malady of sin must not be exposed to the occasion which led to your transgression. If, however, you are unavoidably forced to the place, the person, the time, which have been such occasions, then remember that Jesus is watching for you and praying for you and suffering for you. Say to Him, "Help me, my Agonizing Jesus, to avoid every occasion which I know to be a temptation to sin against Thee."

If you watch outwardly to keep far from you all that which you have reason to think will lead you into sin, you must also watch inwardly. When disease attacks you and prostrates you, the cause is often exterior, but had your constitution been stronger, the infection would not have found entrance or would be successfully resisted. Sin finds entrance into your soul through some chink in your armor. Take that weak constitution into the Garden with Jesus; compare your habits, your disposition, your inclinations with those in His Heart. You will then reform weak habits, improve all dispositions and direct the impulses of your heart towards the sinless Redeemer. In bodily illness, besides avoiding the sources of illness and removing the inner weakness, you must build up within powers of resistance. What does Jesus in Gethsemane advise as a strengthener of the soul? He tells you by word and by example that you must pray. Jesus has just come from the Last Supper where He has fed His Apostles with His own Body and Blood. That sacrament had different effects on all at the First Communion because all had differing dispositions, and the effectiveness of grace depends upon the dispositions of the soul. Some apostles remained apart. Peter, James and John were led closer. When Jesus was captured, most of the apostles fled. Peter followed at a distance and finally denied Jesus. John persevered to the foot of the Cross. Do you not hope to be true to Jesus to the end, avoiding the infection of sin, and by the sacraments gaining supreme health of soul against any future relapse?

Our Fortitude

IN TENTATIONEM. Do you feel now so strong that you can say with St. James, "My brethren, count it all joy when you shall fall into divers temptations, knowing that the trying of your faith produces patience." To bring you that joy is the work of the angel who comforted Jesus in His Agony. After the temptations of Jesus in the desert, angels ministered to Him. When you pray, "Lead us not into temptation," you are asking the consoling help of the angels. They will bring you fortitude and even joy and the assurance that God never permits you to be tempted above your strength.

The example of Jesus will give you even more joy and fortitude. He was led by the Spirit into the desert that He might be tempted. Jesus allows Himself to be handled by the hateful power of the Evil One and became like to us in all things, sin excepted. Have, then, fortitude against the concupiscence of the flesh. Jesus will give you real Bread of life, not stones that lead to death. Have courage if concupiscence of the eyes tempt you. Jesus had all the wealth and power of the world set before Him and drove away the tempter. "The Lord, thy God, thou shalt adore and Him only shalt thou serve." Have fearless daring if tempted to pride, because Jesus on the pinnacle of the Temple spurned the pride and presumption suggested by Satan. Remember, when foul thoughts assail you, that Jesus has already won the fight for you.

The temptation in the Garden was more terrible than the temptations in the desert. The sensitive feelings of Jesus were lashed in prospect before His Body was scourged; His Heart bled before It was opened by the soldier's spear, and His Soul was crucified before He was nailed to the Cross on Calvary. Anticipation is sometimes more terrifying than the reality. In the desert the angel of comfort had to bring food alone; in the Agony the angel must staunch the flow of blood, dispel the black clouds of desolation and comfort a soul sorrowful unto death. The angelic visitation is firm assurance to you that your prayer shall be answered, that your weakness will be fortified, your watchfulness increased and rewarded and your fortitude made like to that of Jesus in His Agony.

Prayer

Sinless Jesus, who for the strengthening of our virtue didst enter into temptation, remove from us, we pray Thee, all weakness of will that with watchful and courageous souls we may, aided by Thy example, have ever the joy of victory over the Evil One. *Amen.*

LEAD US NOT INTO
TEMPTATION

Through breached walls the dread foe courses,
Battling for my heart's control;

Help, Lord, help with Heaven's forces;
Panoply a timorous soul.

>⊱—◆—○—◆—⊰

Eternal Father, I offer Thee the ample satisfaction which Jesus has made to Thy justice for poor sinners upon the tree of the Cross, and I beg of Thee to render efficacious for all sinful souls, on whom sin has inflicted death, the merits of His Precious Blood, so that raised to the life of grace they may glorify Thee for all eternity.

Eternal Father, I offer Thee the ardent desires of the Divine Heart of Jesus in satisfaction for the tepidity and cowardice of Thy chosen people; and I ask of Thee that by the ardent love which caused Him to suffer death it may please Thee to renew the ardour of their tepid hearts in Thy service, and to embrace them with Thy love, so that Thou mayest be eternally loved by them.

Eternal Father, I offer Thee the submission of Jesus to Thy Will, begging of Thee through His merits the consummation of Thy grace, and the accomplishment of all that Thy holy Will desires.

"Saviour of the world, have mercy on us!" "Mother of love, of sorrow and of mercy, pray for us!"

"O Heart of Jesus, I place all my trust in Thee; for, though I fear all things from my weakness, I hope all things from Thy mercy."

But Deliver Us From Evil
Sed Libera Nos A Malo

Deliverance by Faith

SED LIBERA. This petition of the Our Father does not simply repeat the preceding petition in other words; it does not denote the opposite merely; it signifies advance. You have prayed for forgiveness of your sins; you have prayed to be made strong against temptations to sin, and now you say, "Not only from those evils, Our Father, deliver me, but also from all evil whatsoever." The full answer to your prayer will be given to you in Heaven, but faith will reveal to you in this life the good of evil. Jesus has not promised you that you will be freed from all yokes; you shall always have a yoke to carry upon a chafed neck, but Jesus promises that His yoke will be sweeter than the yokes of the world, the flesh and the devil. He assures you that He will be your yoke-fellow, and now in the Garden of Gethsemane, He is fitting that yoke to His bleeding neck and making it smooth and sweeter for you, because He is drawing all things to Himself by the divine and the solacing attraction of His Passion.

The evil that oppresses you and all mankind is indeed a grievous burden. In your litanies you pray the Lord to deliver you from a host of evils, from pestilence, from famine, from war, from death. Who is not appalled at the immense load of evil which God permits upon earth? Faith will remove that fear. "My burden is light," Jesus assures us. All the evils of earth, with the exception of sin, are blessings enriched with heavenly and everlasting good. "For that which is at present momentary and light of our tribulation worketh for us above measure exceedingly an eternal weight of glory." The darkness of your Gethsemane is made bright by the splendor of the reward Jesus wins for you in the Garden. You have seen immense weights rise in the air and fly light as a feather. Take your faith to Jesus in His Agony, and all the burdens of time will take wings and soar to the heights of Heaven.

When Jesus tells you to enter into your Gethsemane and bids you take up your cross daily and follow Him, He promises to be there to steady your tottering steps that you may not fall as He did under His Cross. Every cross that lacerates you, every crucifixion that drives its nails into you and lays open your very heart, is a consoling cross, a life-giving crucifixion already resplendent with the joy of eternal Easter if you will win from Gethsemane a stronger faith.

Deliverance by Character

AOS. You do not pray like a child for whom a mother must do all; you do not pray as one helpless. You pray as one who has grown to the stature of Christ, as one who has put on the armor of Christ. The manhood of Christ and the armor of Christ, that is your character made strong by fortitude against all evil. You may be delivered from all evil by removing the evil, or by making yourself so strong that the evil no longer troubles. A child must be led across a dangerous thoroughfare; an adult does not reach for a parent's hand. Now, you have put fortitude into your soul, fortitude to bear all sufferings. Along the thoroughfare of life pass inclemency of weather, disasters on sea and land, a veritable procession of diseases, but you are not dismayed, you have been in the Garden with Jesus and you step bravely across the paths of storms and calamities to the security Jesus prepares for you in Heaven.

Your fortitude of character is stronger still. It not only bears with suffering, it also seeks suffering. "If any one will follow me," said Jesus, "he must take up his cross." You know that character is good will made strong, and you know that you make a power strong by using it. Your will is transformed to character, not in idleness, not in floating down stream, but in pulling hard against the current. Jesus denied Himself, fasting in the desert; Jesus denied Himself spending the night in prayer. Jesus prayed in agony while the weaker characters of His Apostles went to sleep. For vanity or for health of body thousands practice voluntary self-denial. For virtue and for health of soul, you will have to have the fortitude to seek suffering. You can be delivered from some evils only by prayer and fasting.

Are you courageous enough to ask for still greater fortitude of character and with the saints even love suffering? St. Francis of Assisi in the zeal of his fortitude espoused privation and took poverty as his lady. St. Theresa felt that she must suffer or there would be no more life for her. The saintly Cure of Ars found his delight where worldlings found pain. These and countless others followed the example of Jesus, who having joy set before him, embraced the Cross. You are delivered most assuredly from all the sinless evils of time, if with Jesus and His saints you have the fortitude which endures, which seeks, which loves suffering.

Deliverance by Holiness

MALO. To equip your character fully and insure it against evil, you should add to fortitude the other cardinal virtues which Jesus taught through life and practiced perfectly in His Agony and Passion. Temperance will deliver you from much evil of body. When Jesus fasted from the Last Supper to His death, when loss of blood and gaping wounds forced Him to give pitiful voice to His torturing desire for drink, then

by His hunger and thirst He won for you
deliverance from the evils of food and drink
that have filled the world with wickedness
and death. The scourging of the innocent and
naked body of Jesus teaches man the lesson of
purity, and His blood is the wine that makes
virgins. All the evils which come from the
abuse of man's appetites, were before Jesus in
His Agony and for you and for all He prayed
and He merited deliverance. "Our Father,
deliver us from evil; Our Jesus, deliver us
from bodily ill by Thy Divine temperance."

Evils of mind are in a way worse than evils
of body. False principles, pagan rejection of
the ideals of Christ have led to intemperance,
to impurity, to violated marriage vows and
to the homes wrecked by divorce. The cardinal virtue of Christian prudence will deliver
mankind from the evils of debased morals. In
the soul which knows and wills is the image
of God; the body retains only vestiges of divinity. Imagine then the horror in the mind of
Jesus when he beheld the divine image of the
human soul disfigured by falsehood, by rebel-
lion against law, by irreligion, by standards of
life not far removed from the lowest animals.

Deliver us from evil! Put into us the mind which was in Christ Jesus, and by His divine prudence free us from all bad judgments.

With body and mind protected from evil, you will need finally deliverance of will. All your virtues do indeed strengthen your will, steeling it with the firm resolve to do your duty at all costs. Yet that virtue which gives everyone and everything its due, justice to creatures, to fellow-man, to God, governs the other virtues and is your guarantee that every act of your free will is responding fully and perfectly to duty. The cardinal virtues are practiced in every good act, bravely, temperately, prudently and justly performed, but justice sees to it that even the cardinal virtues reach their due measure and perfection. God's infinite justice was forced to exact an infinite atonement for the infinite offence of sin. Revelation from Genesis to Apocalypse echoes from page to page with justice. The justice of Jesus abounds, and though one bead in the sweat of blood were enough to fulfill all justice, He permitted His Heart to bathe His body in that saving dew. If you cannot be as generous as Jesus in His Agony, at least you can join with Him in the Our Father He is enacting and uttering in the Garden. Deliver us from evil; free our wills from all evil by the divine justice which God exacted and which Thou, dear Jesus, didst pay a thousand times over.

Prayer

Infinitely merciful God, eternal Font of all good, regard with loving pity the trials of Thy children, and when Thy kind Providence so orders, grant that with our life freed from all evil and our souls vested in every virtue, we may be delivered from the sorrows of earth unto the endless bliss of Heaven. *Amen*.

DELIVER US FROM EVIL

Yoke with us, Lord, in life's plowing;
Raze to root all choking weeds,

And with full-hand, fruitful sowing
Leave no soil for cockle seeds!

"My Jesus, Mercy!"

"Jesus, Son of David, have mercy on me'

"O Lord, God Almighty, who permittest evil to draw good therefrom, hear our humble prayers, and grant that we remain Faithful to Thee unto death. Grant us also through the intercession of most holy Mary the strength ever to conform ourselves to Thy most holy will!"

So Be It
Amen

Amen of Man

AMEN. You have said the Our Father with Jesus. He lived the Our Father in Gethsemane, and you have tried to live it again with Him. Now you say Amen to every syllable of that enacted prayer. With the one word, Amen, you resume all your desires and thoughts. Amen puts you on an eminence from which you can review every step of your pilgrimage. The sacred sounds of the Lord's Prayer still echo in your ears. The fragrance exhaled from a score of blossoms freshens and pervades the air about you. Yet you have not exhausted the treasures of that divine prayer. The words of God are as inexhaustibly rich as God Himself. You would, if that were possible, sum up in your Amen all the meaning of the Our Father and all the visions which inspired God's saints when they meditated upon the Lord's prayer. Most of all you would wish and earnestly pray that you might have before your mind all the revelations of darkness and of light, of sin, of reparation, of eternal reward which Jesus beheld when He lived through the Our Father in the Garden Agony.

Amen is a ratification as well as a resumé. By that word you make an inventory; by that word you sign a contract. Amen is your signature to the precious document which Jesus hands to you. You promise to pay what you saw was a debt due to yourself, your neighbor, and your God. You volunteer for the King and in Amen you proclaim that you will not be a traitor, Before God's altar you enter upon an espousal higher and more lasting than any human wedding. Your fervent Amen is even more earnest and heartfelt than the "I do" with which bride and groom bind themselves for life. When Jesus said in the Garden, "Thy will be done," He pronounced His Amen. You witness His signature. You know that His credit is good. You see Him struggle and win for His Father. The Church is the Bride of Christ, and the betrothal was renewed and confirmed by the Agony and Passion in which Jesus gave to His Bride the shining purity of justification.

Your Amen is a resolve, far indeed from the adamant resolution of Jesus, but still a resolve. With the Amen of review and of solemn contract, you join the sincerity of love. Your Amen echoes in your heart when it is heard upon your lips. Had you the Heart of Christ there would be heard an echo whose reverberations are never to cease. Yet in very truth the resolution of your heart has an eternal consequence. The grace of your Amen is a gift from the Heart that bled in Gethsemane, and that grace is to persist forever in just retribution for ingratitude or in the everlasting glory of your gratefully fulfilled Amen.

Amen of Jesus

OU have to question yourself, when you say Amen, whether you mean what you say, but when Jesus says Amen, you have the assurance of infinite truth that His Amen is no lip sound but a soul reality. The first meaning of Amen is to adopt as your own what has been said by another, the second meaning is the solemn assurance

that the statement which is found with Amen,
singly or doubled, is undoubtedly true. Our
Lord in the Gospels frequently makes use of
Amen, often when a difficulty is urged or felt
against what is said. Amen is a foundation of
rock for your faith, You may feel then most
certain that Jesus whispered the Amen of
divine assurance to strengthen your faith in
every truth of the Our Father.

Words with Jesus are sacramental;
they do what they say. Jesus liked prompt
performance. The Prodigal said, "I will
arise and go" and he arose and went. The
Roman officer is approved of who gave
orders to come and go and found them
obeyed at once. Mary heard the words of Incarnation and went in haste upon her Visitation. The Magi reported, "We have seen
the star in the East and have come to adore."
The Amen of Jesus put faith and its blessings
in the souls of all believers. Upon the Cross
Jesus said to the repentant thief, "Amen, I
say to thee, this day thou shalt be with me in
paradise." You may therefore be certain that
Jesus utters the same Amen for you in His
Agony and Passion and that as He did what

the thief asked, so also for you He will this day do what you ask in the Our Father.

Your Amen is ratified by the sincere resolve of your heart; you have not been compelled to write your name in your own blood to the contract you have made. Jesus put His Amen into rubrics that all who run may read. You have not stamped upon your agreement a seal, cutting and heavy, like the sharp outlines driven into red sealing-wax. Martyrs are witnesses, and make good their testimony by shedding their blood. Jesus put into act the Amen of martyrdom. Upon the Cross he cried, "It is consummated," that is the Amen to the life of Jesus. With that word Jesus put the key-stone of completion into the great arch that spans creation with its bases in antecedent and subsequent infinity.

Amen of God

ST. JOHN in his Apocalypse calls "Amen a faithful and true witness and the beginning of the creation of God."

In some versions of Scripture Amen is translated by the Latin Fiat. "So let it be" is very like "Let it be done," and if Amen figured in Creation, so also will it figure in the consummation of all things. God is the beginning and the end, the alpha and the omega.

God is the Divine Amen. His omnipotence, His truth assures us that your Our Father and all your prayers will be fully answered as shall be best for you. The evils of time against which you pray, shall lose their gloom in the light of eternity. The Easter that came to the body of Jesus will come to every redeemed body, bearing the wounds of faithful service to Jesus. God will say Amen to your agony as He did to the Agony in the Garden, and you will rise with Jesus to eternal Easter.

God will say Amen for your soul also and to the beauty of your glorified body shall be added glorifying truth whose complete embodiment is God. The hidden truths of all science which have enraptured mankind, will find full revelation in God. What faith reveals darkly shall be seen face to face. Upon the lofty heights of Heaven are found the tabernacles which the Apostles wished to build upon Thabor. "The hour is now come," said Jesus after his Agony; "Sleep and take your rest." With a difference of meaning, but with the same assurance, God will say Amen, the hour is now come. Sleep and take your rest in the satisfying contemplation of all truth, an eternal rest won for you by the sleepless watching and suffering of your agonized Jesus.

The greatest Amen which God will utter is the completion of love. St. John in the Apocalypse voices for us the hymn of love chanted by the blessed in Heaven and note how the chant begins and ends: "Amen. Benediction and glory and wisdom and thanksgiving, honor and power and strength to our God forever and ever. Amen." The greatest craving of man's heart is love, and that craving is divinely implanted in you that you may be ever restless and yearning until you rest in God Himself Who will satisfy the longing, aching, burning heart which is ever intent upon seeking love and ever disappointed in its human objects. God is love, and the only thing which God hates is sin. When Jesus removed sin by His Agony and Passion, He made ready your heart for the coming of the Holy Spirit, the Person of the

Holy Trinity, who is the Love of Father and Son. When therefore God says Amen to the Our Father in Gethsemane, He writes the end to the Book of Life. All accounts are closed and settled, and with glorified body, glorified mind and glorified will you shall begin the real business of your existence, eternal enjoyment. Amen you say, and Amen cries Jesus and Amen proclaims God, Our Father.

Prayer

Increase within us, loving and lovable Lord Jesus, the sincerity of our faith that every petition and promise which we make in the prayer Thou hast taught us, may through the merits of the Agony find perfect fulfillment here in the happiness of earth and hereafter in the felicity of our Father. *Amen*.

AMEN

Christ's Amen is our salvation;
Man's Amen its echoing;

Hosts of Heaven in elation
God's Amen forever sing.

The Divine Praises

Blessed be God.

Blessed be His holy Name.

Blessed be Jesus Christ, true God and true man.

Blessed be the Name of Jesus.

Blessed be His most Sacred Heart.

Blessed be His most Precious Blood.

*Blessed be Jesus in the Most
Holy Sacrament of the Altar.*

*Blessed be the great Mother of God,
Mary most holy.*

Blessed be her holy and immaculate conception.

Blessed be the name of Mary. Virgin and Mother.

Blessed be St. Joseph, her most chaste spouse.

Blessed be God in His angels and in His saints.

"May the Heart of Jesus, be loved everywhere!"

*"Reward, O Lord, with eternal life all those
who do us good for Thy Name's sake!"*

*"Jesu, to Thee I live—Jesu, to Thee I die
—Jesu, Thine I am in life and in death!"*

Hymn to Christ the King

Through God's eternal kinship Thou hast won
   Thy crown divine:
With Thee we hold allegiance, Christ the King;
For Thee we stand unconquered on the
   soul's long battle line;
To Thee the spoils of victory we bring.

   Our King in kind words spoken;
      our King in duty done;

   Our King in worship chanted;
      our King in silent prayer;

   Our King for homes unbroken,
      our King for priest and nun;

   Our King for soiled or sainted,
      King ever, everywhere!

We build Thee royal palaces
   where loyal voices sing;
We grace Thee with the glories of all art,
But higher we enthrone Thee, kindest
   Lord and loving King,
Forever on the love of every heart.

Chorus: Our King in kind words spoken;
*   our King in duty done;*

Our King in worship chanted;
*   our King in silent prayer;*

Our King for homes unbroken,
*   our King for priest and nun;*

Our King for soiled or sainted,
*   King ever, everywhere!*

By all the rights of conqueror
*   Thou art our King and Friend;*
Thy ransom is far richer than our loss,
*   Thy hands and heart tho' wounded sore*
*   fought onward to the end,*
The victor on the red field of the Cross.

*   Chorus: Our King. . .*

By royal right still nobler and by right all rights
above Upon Thy brow is placed Thy diadem;
Had we no other title, then ten thousand hearts
*   of love*
Would crown Thee King for all Thy love of them.

*   Chorus: Our King . . .*

APPENDIX

"The Holy Hour"

Note: These indulgences were valid when this booklet was originally published in 1935. The current regulations state that a "partial indulgence" is granted to the faithful who devoutly take part in the pious exercises of a public novena before the feast of Pentecost. (Enchiridion of Indulgences, 1968, No. 34). (Partial indulgences are no longer measured in "days" and "years.") —Publisher, 2010.

There are three practices of the Holy Hour, specially authorized and indulgenced by the Church. The first is wholly Eucharistic and is made in public or private for one hour on Holy Thursday, Corpus Christi, and any Thursday of the year in commemoration of the institution of the Blessed Sacrament. Any pious exercise during the hour (meditation, vocal prayers, etc.) suffices for the indulgences. The indulgences are: 1. Plenary for Holy Thursday with Confession and Communion on the day or during the week following; 2. Plenary for Corpus Christi on the same conditions; 3. Three Hundred Days every

Thursday of the year. (Beringer, *Les Indulgences*. French authorized translation, 1905, Vol L, 371.) Many associations of the Church practice such a Holy Hour in honor of the Blessed Sacrament. Among them may be mentioned the Archconfraternity of the most Blessed Sacrament (*Beringer, II*, 128), the Archconfraternity of Perpetual Adoration (*ibid* 130, 133), the Association of Priests Adorers (*ibid* 452), the Priests Eucharistic League. The Archconfraternity of the Eucharistic Heart of Jesus (*ibid* 480) prescribes half an hour weekly. All of these devotions are indulgenced for the members of such societies if the conditions required in each case are complied with.

The second kind of Holy Hour was instituted in accordance with a revelation related by Blessed Margaret Mary. It consists of an hour of prayer in union with the agony of Our Lord in the Garden, in order to appease the anger of Our Lord and to win graces for sinners. This hour is made by members of the Archconfraternity of the Holy Hour, an organization founded by Father Debrosse, S.J., at Paray-Le-Monial. It has been approved and extended by different popes and in 1911 the Archconfraternity at Paray-Le-Monial was empowered to aggregate confraternities anywhere in the world. In order to gain the indulgences members must have their names inscribed on an official register. In the case of all religious communities, it is sufficient to have the community itself inscribed once for all. To gain the plenary indulgence granted on each occasion, with the usual conditions, the members must pray for any hour from Thursday afternoon to Friday morning in union with Jesus in Agony, for the purpose of appeasing God's wrath against sinners and in reparation for sinners. This Holy Hour is concerned with the Passion rather than with the Blessed Sacrament. (*Beringer, II,* 144).

The third Holy Hour is an extension of this second one. First every individual member of the Apostleship of Prayer may gain the plenary indulgence granted to the members of the Confraternity of the Holy Hour without being registered in that Confraternity provided he fulfills the conditions, namely an hour of meditation or vocal prayer on the Passion at the time designated, with Confession and Communion. Secondly, this privilege was extended in 1875 by Leo XIII, and members of the Apostleship who practice the hour in common, may now make it on any day or hour once a week. (*Beringer, II, 202.*) In this rescript occur the following words: "It has been reported to us that many of the Associates of the Apostleship mentioned, called together by the directors according to the statutes of the League, are wont to assemble on certain hours and days in churches or chapels to perform in honor of the Most Sacred Heart of Jesus or of the August Sacrament of the Altar the pious exercise of adoration and reparation belonging to the devotion of the Holy Hour." The words here cited do not restrict the prayers and meditations to the Passion alone, but include exercises in honor of the Sacred Heart of the Blessed Sacrament, such would seem to be the general custom now. The Holy Hour, which was originally concerned with the Agony in the Garden, has grown to comprehend all the Passion the Sacred Heart, and the Holy Eucharist. In practice the faithful should be recommended to entertain thoughts of sympathy with Christ suffering, of hatred for sin, of reparation to Christ for the ingratitude and indifference of mankind.